I am Shudu

*Finding my voice,
knowing my strength*

First published by Jacana Media (Pty) Ltd in 2023

10 Orange Street, Sunnyside
Auckland Park 2092, South Africa
+2711 628 3200
www.jacana.co.za

Text and illustrations © Shudufhadzo Musida, 2023
All rights reserved.

ISBN 978-1-4314-3383-4

Illustrated by Chantelle & Burgen Thorne
Set in Cambria 13/24pt
Job no. 004050
Printed and bound by Tandym Print

See a complete list of Jacana titles at www.jacana.co.za

SHUDUFHADZO MUSIDA

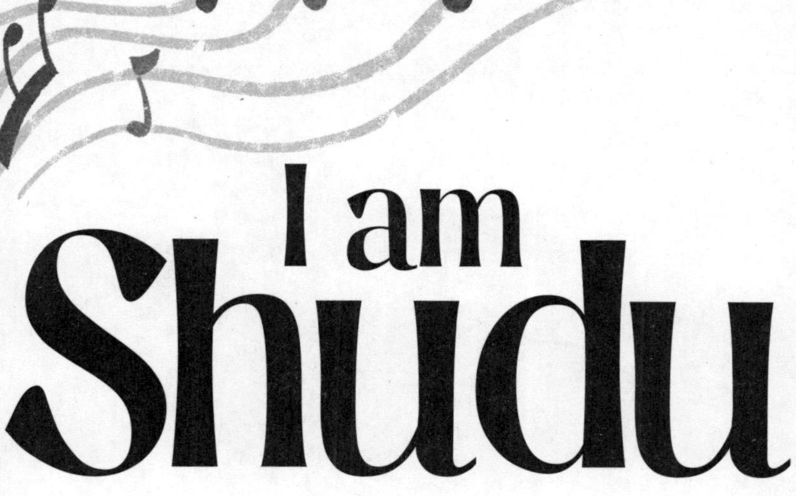

I am Shudu

*Finding my voice,
knowing my strength*

JACANA
CHILDREN'S
BOOKS

Illustrated by Chantelle & Burgen Thorne

I have often read the saying, "We are our ancestors' wildest dreams." My late grandfather, Vho Elias Musida, saw his wildest dreams through me. I dedicate this book to him, the man who allowed me to be and loved me most beautifully and purely. I look forward to reading you this book outside at home under the stars.
Shudufhadzo Musida

One of our favourite quotes is this one: "Be kind. Everyone you meet is fighting a hard battle." It's truer now than ever. Remember, kindness is a superpower!
Chantelle & Burgen Thorne

Shudu
Gugu
Lydie
Sihle

Contents

Chapter 1
The beginning

Shudu loved playing with her cousin Thivhadini. Thivhadini was the same age as Shudu, born a month before her. They lived in the village of Ha-Vhangani in Limpopo, went to school together and were rarely apart.

Sometimes they grabbed their skipping ropes and skipped in the street. Sometimes, as they played, they heard the other children shouting. Shudu knew it was because the old man was leading his cows to graze in the fields.

"Shudufhadzo Abigail Musida, where have you been?" her aunt called out. "Your mother has been looking for you."

Shudu's mother was sitting on the couch and Shudu sat down next to her.

"Why do you look so sad, Mama?"

"I've found a new job, my lovely child."

"But then you should look happy, Mama."

"I look sad because my job is in another town and that means I have to go away."

"Where are you going?"

"To Secunda in Mpumalanga. When I find a nice home for us there, I will send for you. In the meanwhile, you will stay with your aunt."

Shudu's eyes filled with tears. "But Mama…"

Just then her Aunt Cecilia walked into the room.
"You will be all right. I am here. So is your
great-grandmother, Gugu. Your mom will come
to visit as often as she can. Now, dry your eyes
and help your mother pack."

The days and months flew by and Shudu was
happy living at Aunt Cecilia's house as it meant
she could share a room with Thivhadini.

It was Saturday and her grandmother was home from Johannesburg.

"Aunt Cecilia, I'm just going to visit Granny."

"Make sure your teeth are clean and your hair is brushed. **You know how strict Vho-Marandela is**."

Shudu nodded.

"Good girl, then off you go."

Shudu had great respect for her Granny and was even a little afraid of her. Granny was very strict and Shudu made absolutely sure she always behaved perfectly.

Granny asked the same questions every time:
"I hope you are working hard at school. Are you
helping your auntie in the house? **Are you
reading a book every day?**"

"Come, sit with me, my child."

Shudu nodded and smiled. "Thanks, Granny.
It's lovely to have you home."

"Taste some of my putu and stew, my child,"
said Granny. "Let me know what you think.
I will be having it for dinner."

They sat and chatted about all the things that
had happened while Granny had been away.

Shudu tasted Granny's food.

"You must have some more, Shudu."

"Just a little, please." She did not want
to disappoint her Granny. **She did
not like disappointing
anyone**.

Then it was time to visit her
great-grandmother, Gugu.

Chapter 2
Story time

The best part of Shudu's day was when she visited her great-grandmother, Gugu. **Gugu was the person she loved most in the whole world**. She was known as Vho-Nwanzeru and was one of the wise elders of the village.

"Gugu, I am here." She kissed her Gugu's wrinkled cheek and held her hand.

"Hello, my child."

"What are you doing today, Gugu?"

"I am making muroho wa thanga for our family lunch. I've taught many people how to make it. The pumpkin leaves and onions are ready and now I'm going to grind the nuts. While I do that, I will tell you a story. This will be an old story."

Gugu

"I love your old Venda stories, Gugu."

"I know, my child; I enjoy telling you about the great women in my village who helped shape the way for so many of us."

"One day, I am going to be a great woman, just like Beyoncé. She is such a great entertainer and is so beautiful." said Shudu.

"I see," Gugu smiled. "I want you to be a great woman too. Just remember to always be yourself. **Beauty comes from within**, and that means taking care of yourself on the inside, then you will be beautiful on the outside."

"But you are extra special. Your birthday is on the same day and month as Nelson Mandela," said Gugu.

"Mama always reminds me. She says one day I will also do something great like he did. I hope I will."

"You will," Gugu said. **"There are many different ways to make a change in the world."**

Shudu loved her family lunches on Saturdays, and they would go on for hours. She would sit with her Gugu, listening, taking in the stories of her family and of life in the village of Ha-Vhangani. She watched Gugu's brown, lined hands as she worked at the large mortar and pestle in her backyard.

"Next week, you will come with me to the meeting of the elders. You know I always remind you how important it is for you to go to school. Our village will grow in wealth and wisdom when more of our children, especially our girls, are educated."

Shudu nodded. "I am working hard, Gugu."

She liked going to the meetings. She sat quietly and listened carefully.

"And now we must talk about tomorrow, Shudu. You and Thivhadini must come with me to church this Sunday. I have told the minister that you are coming, and he asked that you sing a song."

"Oh yes! I would love to sing, Gugu."

"You must sing the song 'Khonani' because everybody loves that one."

"That's my favourite song as well, this is my best part…

On Sundays, Shudu would go to church with one of her grandmothers. If Granny was home, they would argue a little about who was taking her. They were both very proud of Shudu.

The days passed quickly for Shudu, life in the village was peaceful.

Then, one day, when she got home, she heard Aunt Cecilia shouting. Her aunt ran inside waving a letter. "I've been looking for you everywhere. Your mother has sent for you. It is time for you to go and live with her in Secunda."

Shudu took a deep breath to calm herself.
She would be very sad to leave her family
and the village, but she was going to be with
her mother at last.

Chapter 3
Mixed feelings
24

Shudu stood in front of the door. Her heart
pounded as her mother handed her the keys.

**"You can open the door to your new
home**," she said.

Shudu stepped inside and glanced around.
"Oh Mama, it's lovely."

Her mother hugged her and held her close.
"In the evenings, we can relax and watch
television. We will have a wonderful time
together. Come, let me show you
your bedroom. To celebrate, I will
make your favourite dinner."

"Muroho wa thanga!"
they both said at the
same time and laughed.

The next day, her mother took her to her new school. As they walked, her mother talked.

"Now, at last, you are with me in Mpumalanga. Do you know what Mpumalanga means?"

Shudu shook her head. "It means 'the place where the sun rises'. And I hope that when that sun rises it will shine on us."

It only took one day for Shudu to feel that the sun did not shine on her. She just did not fit in. She spoke Venda. Everyone else spoke Siswati or isiZulu. The girls laughed at her when she tried to learn to speak English.

"Your English is bad. **Maybe you shouldn't speak at all**," someone shouted.

"**You don't belong here**. Go back to where you came from," said another girl.

Shudu did not know what to do. "I can't tell Mama. She works so hard at the bank. I can't tell anyone," she said to herself.

The next day the girls started pushing her in the playground. "You come from some small town that nobody knows. Go back there."

"But I don't come from there," she lied, hoping they would stop. They did not.

Shudu had beautiful hair that she grew out. Sometimes, when she slept on her back, the hair on the back of her head would be flat. This, of course, was new fodder for the mean girls.

"**Stadium, stadium**," they giggled to her face. "You should have eyes in the back of your head to see what you look like!" That made them laugh even louder.

In an act of defiance, **Shudu shaved her head**. It did not help. Unfortunately, this just brought a new way for her to be tormented by the children.

"Ha ha, Shudu, your forehead is so shiny. Why is your head so big?" asked one boy. "Look at you! You've got a long forehead."

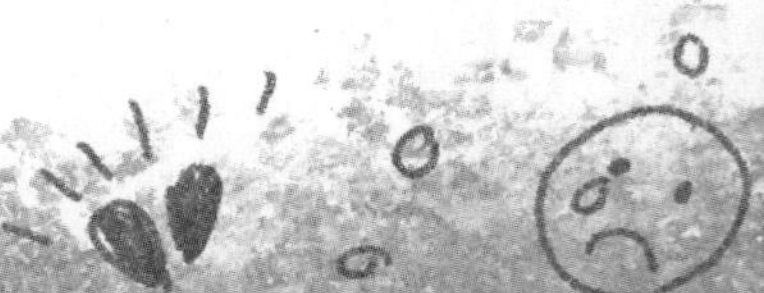

They laughed so loudly that Shudu had
to walk away quickly.

"Big head! Big head!" they shouted.

Shudu felt like she was nothing. From being so happy in Ha-Vhangani, now she wished that a hole would open in the ground. She wanted to fall in and disappear. Shudu felt like her heart would break. She missed her cousin Thivhadini and her Gugu. She missed home. **She felt so alone**.

Then came the devastating news that her Gugu had died.

Shudu cried for weeks and weeks. She was heartbroken.

She felt more alone than ever.

Chapter 4
A friend in need

Every day was hard for Shudu. During break, she would quickly run to the back of the school and hide there. "Don't look here. Please don't find me," she whispered over and over again. "Why can't I be like the other girls? **What's wrong with me?**" She could not stop crying.

This was the start of many years of bullying. The girls and boys around her were mean and spiteful and seemed determined to make her feel bad about herself. Somehow, Shudu felt deeply ashamed. "**What have I done?**"

She felt that she had caused the girls to treat her this way. She thought she was responsible for their meanness and that things would get better if she tried harder.

"If I can change
and be a different
person maybe things
will get better."

And then one day things did change.

She was thinking of her Gugu moving back and forth grinding the nuts. Then she thought of her grandmother and her cousin Thivhadini, and her eyes filled with tears.

A girl came over and sat down next to her. **"Don't cry. Please, don't cry."**

"Go away, Yvette," said Shudu. "Those girls will be nasty to you as well."

"So, let them. I don't care."

Shudu looked up. "You don't care?"

"They're not very nice and **I don't want to be friends with bullies**. I would never say such awful things to anyone. Nobody should say things like that."

From that day Shudu and Yvette were the best of friends.

Shudu finally understood what it was like to have someone to talk to. At last, she had found someone who was kind to her. From that day in Grade 5 all the way through to Grade 7 the girls were together.

They were both looking forward to high school. They sat and planned all the things they would do, and which sports they would choose.

"Swimming! I hope they have a pool or take us to one."

"I just hope we have nice girls in our class," said Shudu.

Then they got the news. Their parents had decided to send them to different schools. Yvette and Shudu were heartbroken that they were to be separated.

At her new school, Shudu was back in a class with some of the children who had bullied her.

Once again, she dreaded going to school because the bullying started again.

"Why didn't you go to another school?" shouted one of them.

"Don't you know we don't want you here!" said another.

"No. Not again, please, not again," Shudu said to herself. "Why does this happen to me? Why can't they be friendly instead of bullying me? What have I done wrong?"

She went back into herself, feeling unsure and alone.

But then something wonderful happened.
She met a girl named Sihle.

Slowly over the weeks Sihle and Shudu
became great friends. Shudu learnt to trust her.

**"I am so lucky to have found a friend
like you**, Shudu," smiled Sihle.

"What are you talking about! I felt so alone
before I met you. And I missed my family
terribly," confided Shudu.

"I'm lucky to have my family with me here,
yours are so far away."

"Exactly, Sihle, we don't even know our
neighbours here – in my village you know
everyone."

Shudu often had to prepare orals for her English lesson at school. She would practice at home many times to make sure she knew it well. Just thinking about having to stand up in front of the whole class to say a speech was scary for her.

"I always feel terrified, I am not sure I can do this," said Shudu.

"I'll be there to support you, Shudu, try to stay calm."

Shudu was so anxious that she felt like she
stumbled over her words and forgot parts
of the oral.

"**I got stage fright**, and couldn't think
properly. Even worse, I looked like a ball
of sweat and my body was itching. It's so
embarrassing!"

"I am proud of you for trying, Shudu. That
is all that matters – that you did your best!"

One day Sihle called Shudu.

"Look what I've got," and she handed Shudu
a present. "**Happy birthday, Shudu**."

Shudu couldn't believe it. "This is the first
birthday present I've been given by a friend."
She had tears in her eyes.

"Go on. Open it." Sihle was jumping
up and down with excitement.
"See, it's a picture frame. Turn it over."

Shudu turned it over and saw the loving
words her friend had written.

"**Oh, thank you, thank you**." She could
hardly speak. She was so happy she wanted
to sing like she had when she was a little girl.

Shudy
For my special friend
I love I you

Chapter 5
A new home

Everything changed again when Shudu was 15 years old.

"Shudu, my darling, we are moving to Randburg. I have been able to get a good job in Johannesburg. I hope it will be a much better place to live."

Shudu kissed her mother. "**Wow. That's great, Mama**," she said. "We should celebrate."

"We will. This evening we will go out and have the best meal ever."

"Mmm ... pizza?" And her mother laughed happily.

"Another town, another school." Shudu was nervous. **"I hope there are no girls who are nasty,"** she said softly as she went to her bedroom. Her stomach did flip-flops as she thought about it.

Once again they moved. The place was so big that it seemed that no one spoke to each other. Shudu felt more isolated and alone. Leaving Sihle was hard.

"I can't tell my mom how I feel, I need to figure things out myself," she thought.

"Oh, how I miss my Gugu. I wish she was here to talk to."

Shudu would sing "Khonani" to herself, imagining she was back in the village with Thivhadini and her Gugu. That would make her feel a little stronger.

On the first day at Bryanston High School Shudu made a promise to herself. "Never again. Nobody will have the chance to bully me. I will not make any friends. **I will spend all my time studying**."

At lunch break she realised there was a girl standing in front of her.

"Shudu, the headmaster wants to see you."

He was standing on the field with a group of girls. "Shudufhadzo let me introduce you to these students. I will leave you with them."

"We would like to show you around the school," one of the girls said.

"No thanks. I'm quite happy to find my own way around." She turned and walked away.

The girls were surprised.

"But … the…"

"Really, I can look after myself, thanks."

They stood whispering to themselves.

Every day Shudu spent every spare moment in the library. She even snuck her sandwiches in there and ate them at lunchtime. In her heart, she felt utterly alone. She wanted to fit in but wouldn't make friends with anyone. Her world grew smaller and smaller.

"I wish I could be like them," she said. "But **I just don't want to be hurt again.**"

This went on for three or four months and she felt very lonely. **Her world was mostly silent**.

All she did was go to school, study hard and help her mother around the house. She also spent her afternoons alone at home waiting for her mother to return from work. Sometimes she cooked.

One day in Grade 10, Shudu was walking to her next class when she saw a girl walking down the passage towards her. The girl had the most infectious laugh. For the first time in a long time, Shudu felt that she wanted to make friends with someone.

"**What is that girl's name?** The one with the braids, tied in a bun."

"Oh, that's Lydie," someone said.

Then a short while later in maths class, everything changed. She sat down next to Lydie.

"**I hate maths**," Lydie whispered. "Just, please wake me up if I fall asleep."

Shudu giggled and very soon they started whispering to each other.

"Lydie and Shudu, would you both like to share your interesting conversation with us, or perhaps the headmaster? No? Then I suggest you keep it for lunch break."

They did and every lunch break they were huddled together. From Grade 10 to Grade 12 the girls were the best of friends. They also spent a lot of time together after school. They played hockey and joined quite a few school activities.

Shudu started to trust again, to understand that the bullying was not her fault, that she was a good person.

Chapter 6

A new page

"I think I am going to join the choir; **I love singing**."

"You should," said Lydie. "You can sing, girl!"

Shudu laughed.

So Shudu joined the choir. Soon she was invited to audition for the provincial choir. She was also invited to take part in the Eisteddfod.

"You seem to be practicing your music a lot, Shudu," said her mother. "It's lovely to see you so committed to your choir group."

"I love it, Mama, and I've been invited to try out for the provincial choir."

But when the time came to try out for the provincial choir, she did not. **She felt she was not good enough** and thought she would be rejected.

Then one day when Shudu was practicing her singing for the choir, a girl passed and heard her...

"You should think about performing in the school show, Shudu. **Your voice is amazing**."

"Really, I get terrible stage fright. I am not sure; I'll think about it."

"Come on, Shudu," encouraged Lydie. "You've always had a dream to be on the stage and perform."

"I ... I ... I'm not sure Lydie."

"You love Beyoncé. She is so strong; just imagine you are her on that stage!"

"I know, I am obsessed with her. Have you heard her cover of 'Crazy', she is incredible."

After a little more persuasion from Lydie,
Shudu bravely wrote her name down.
She spent the rest of the time practising
the two songs she had chosen.

The day of the school show arrived. She could
feel butterflies in her stomach. Her hands were
sweaty, and she kept walking up and down
backstage. Eventually it was her turn.

She performed a medley of two songs – "Young Forever" by Jay-Z and then "Crazy" by Gnarls Barkley. How she found the strength to get up onto the stage and sing, she did not know. Her heart thumped loudly, and her hands trembled.

"Wow, Shudu, everybody loved your songs!"

"Thanks, Lydie, I only heard all the clapping and shouting when I had finished singing."

Chapter 7
A bright future

Wits

Shudu felt like a different person.

Whether it was studying, singing or sport …

she loved it all.

Shudu went on to make more friends and

was happy to be around other people.

She started modelling and got used to being

photographed.

"It's like I've just woken up," Shudu said to

Lydie.

"You have, Shudu," said Lydie.

"I am so happy to be myself. I wish my

Gugu could see me now, I miss her every day."

said Shudu.

"Look at us, ten years later, still friends with so many plans and so much to do," said Lydie.

Shudu laughed. "Really??"

"Yes, we can do whatever we want to do."

"Funny you should say that…" said Shudu.

"Why? Go on! Share, girl. What is it you want to do?"

"I want to put my name down for the Miss South Africa Pageant." She said it so fast that Lydie gasped.

"You said it. Now you have to do it."

Lydie was so excited she jumped up and down.

"You just have to do it. But wait..." Her face changed and she frowned. "What about the Covid-19 pandemic? I mean that has turned everything upside down."

"They are doing it online," said Shudu. "It's a meet and greet and a selection."

"Oh wow!" Lydie was amazed. "I really think you could win."

MISS SOUTH AFRICA 2020

And she did.

Shudu went on to win Miss South Africa 2020.

She now works in many ways to help make the
lives of women and girls better. She hopes to
inspire them to use the power of their voices to
make a change.

A note from Shudu

Remember that you must speak to an adult you trust if you are bullied.

This could be a parent, a family member, a teacher, or an elder. A friend cannot solve all your problems, but they can help you feel heard and seen. It is not your fault if something bad happens to you, and nothing is wrong with you. It may feel like it's your fault, but bullying is a reflection of the bully, not you.

Childline – 116

SADAG [The South African Depression and Anxiety Group] 0800 567 567

Photo by Emilynn Rose

About Shudu

Shudufhadzo Musida was crowned Miss South Africa 2020 on 24 October 2020. She received a Bachelor of Social Science degree in philosophy, politics and economics from the University of Pretoria. In 2020 she received her honours in international relations from the University of the Witwatersrand.

Shudufhadzo's focus during her reign as Miss South Africa was on mental health and she launched her successful online series, *Mindful Mondays.*

She is a mental health advocate working alongside various global initiatives such as Global Citizen, United Nations Women's Forum, and important causes within Africa.

She was a goodwill ambassador for the Global Surgery Foundation which focuses on mental health and helps women and children receive life-saving surgeries.

She is the United Nations Population Fund regional champion for East and Southern Africa where she plays a key role in supporting access to sexual and reproductive health and the mental health of women and girls.

In 2022, Shudufhadzo won the *Glamour* Women of the Year Mental Health Game-Changer award. She is a TV host on Afrimaxx broadcasting on the Home Channel in South Africa, focused on the art and design landscape on the African continent.

In 2021, she published her children's picture book *Shudu Finds Her Magic*, which was based on her story about being bullied in school.

Shudu's company, the Masana Group, manages her wellness programmes. Masana means "the rays of the sun" and is a reminder that all will be well. This is the foundation of Shudu's work and this book.

*Shudu working with DKMS Africa to raise awareness
for blood cancer. Photo courtesy of DKMS Africa*

"Khonani"

Khonani yanga yone-yone

Ndi Yesu a ntakadzaho

Kha dzothe thama dzire hone

A huna a mu fhiraho

Mufunwa wa mbilu yanga

Ndi Yesu khonani yanga

This is a Tshivenḓa song which means:

My truest friend is God

who makes me so happy

Out of all my friends

there is no friend better than Him

He is the lover of my soul